Goofy Goats
Guide to Gardening

Elitracewell
Illustrator

by
Theresa F. Teti, DN, MPH

PALMETTO
PUBLISHING
Charleston, SC
www.PalmettoPublishing.com

Copyright © 2024 by Theresa F. Teti, DN, MPH

All rights reserved.

No portion of this book may be reproduced, stored in a retrieval system, or transmitted in any form by any means–electronic, mechanical, photocopy, recording, or other–except for brief quotations in printed reviews, without prior permission of the author.

Paperback ISBN: 979-8-88590-686-9
eBook ISBN: 979-8-88590-687-6

Dedication

This book is dedicated to the developmentally disabled who have a love for gardening and the outdoors.

Theresa F. Teti, DN, MPH
Special Education Teacher
Public Health Educator

Table of Contents

Introduction vii

Tools, Dirt, Planting, Cultivating and Harvesting ix

Chapter One: Tools for home gardening 1

Chapter Two: Fertilizing and Composting 14

Chapter Three: Preparing and cultivating the soil 26

Chapter Four: Planting from Seeds, or Transplanting Starter Plants 31

Chapter Five: Harvesting and preparing for storage 36

Appendix A: Cost of Gardening Supplies 39

Appendix B: Preparing Your Garden for Winter 42

Appendix C: Mapping a garden area to scale 44

Appendix D: Calculate the amount of compost needed ... 45

About the Author 47

Introduction

The need for this workbook was realized while working with a developmentally challenged young man. I noticed that many of his workmates at the Echoing Hope Ranch, Hereford, Arizona would benefit from a written and visual guide to the tasks they perform daily.

The pictures in this workbook are designed to trigger their memory as they work through their daily assignments in the gardens at Echoing Hope Ranch.

My assistant on this project, Eli Tracewell, one of the clients who works at the Echoing Hope Ranch, drew most of the pictures herein. The pictures were drawn on a variety of paper types. They are presented in this book as they appear in the original drawings.

The story is written as dialog might occur between friends. The storyline was added to encourage the target audience to read through the book.

The formatting chosen is both written and pictorial so the reader can follow instructions easily. The Comic Sans MS font was chosen to assist dyslexic individuals to read the text more easily.

I wish to thank the staff at Echoing Hope Ranch, Hereford, Arizona for their support, encouragement, and time while I worked with Eli Tracewell, my illustrator and helper in creation of the concept, drawings and writing of this workbook.

I also wish to thank the Exceptional Student staff at Buena High School, Sierra Vista, Arizona for introducing me to Eli, and for their ongoing encouragement throughout the project.

Tools, Dirt, Planting, Cultivating, Harvesting

Hubert is an inquisitive young man interested in gardening. He started to explore the many mysteries of gardening that had captured his mind by reading easy gardening books with lots of pictures. He learned about the tools he would need to create his garden.

Hubert discovered the common tractor and a barn.

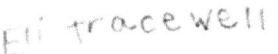

a gardening field ready for planting

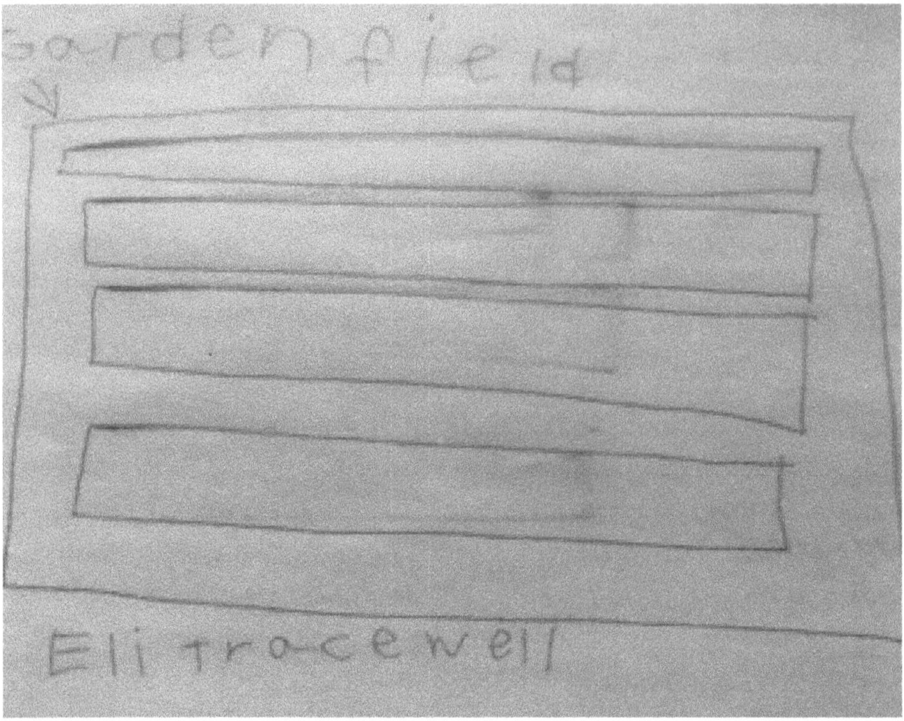

and a garden

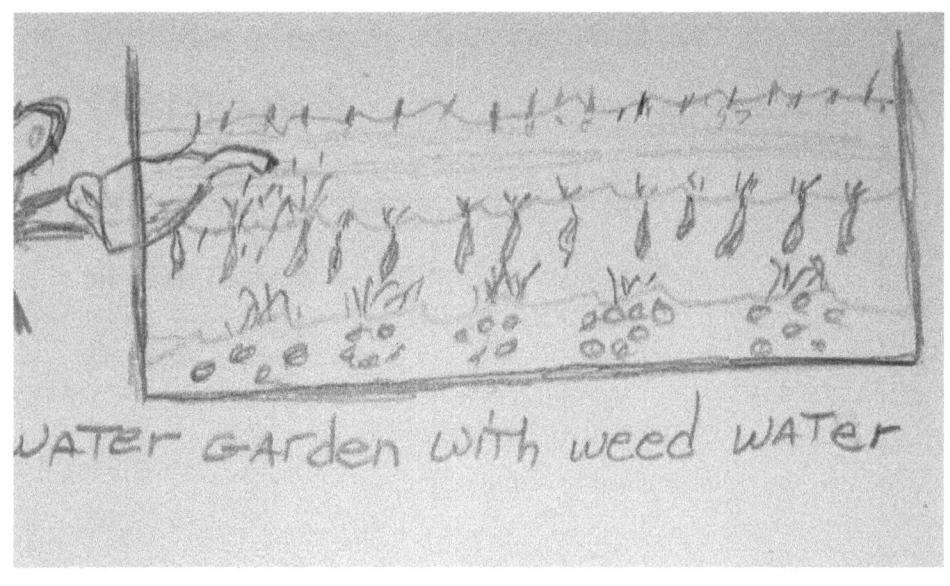

a baby goat

a mama and a baby Pig

and a farm shed

In the shed Hubert found the tools he needed to begin preparing the ground for his garden, and the tools he would need to cultivate his garden.

Chapter One:
Tools for home gardening

In the shed Hubert found big and small tools. He also found other materials he would need to create his very own garden.

    A big tool with very sharp blades, called a Rototiller is used to dig up the ground.

Different size blades are for different soil depth.

Hubert found four types of SHOVELS:

Digging

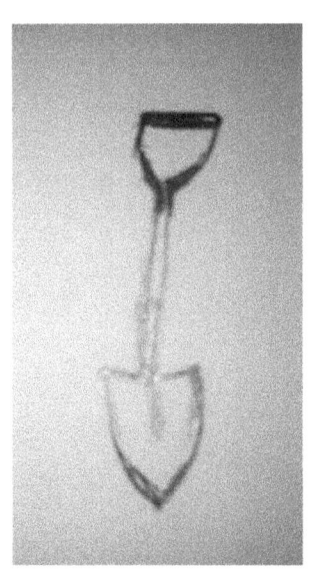

Scooping

Depth

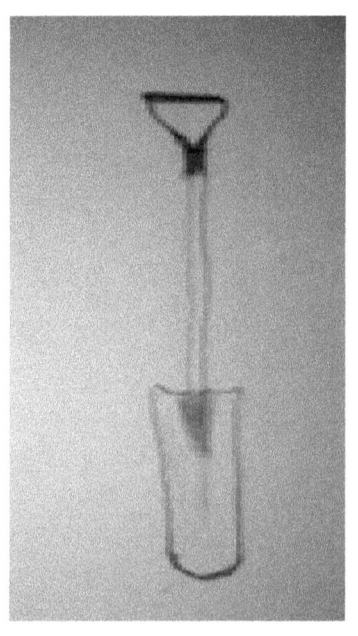

Edging

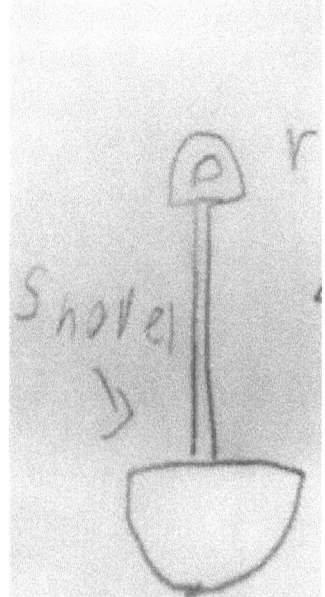

Hubert found 4 types of HOES too. They are used for weeding and smoothing dirt, and for digging and uprooting tough weeds.

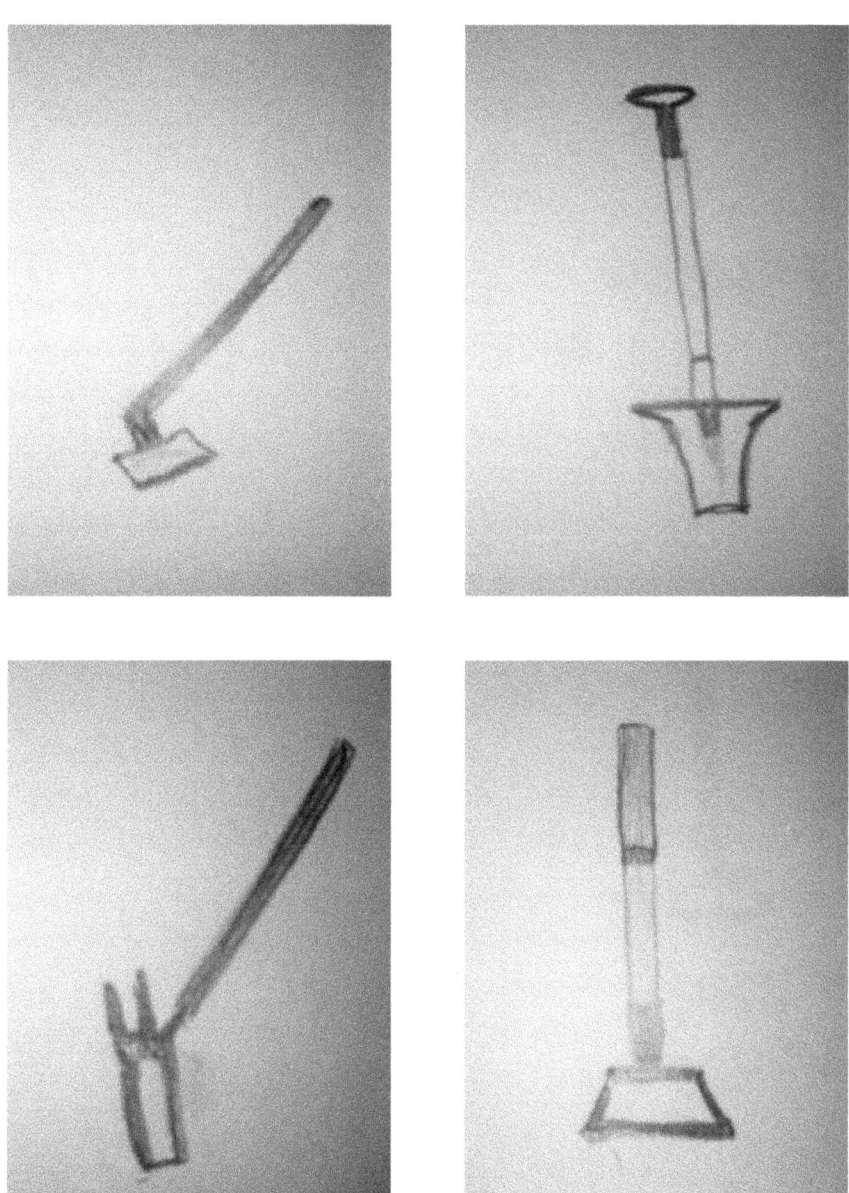

He also found two kinds of RAKES, and a Pitchfork.

Rock & Debris Rake   Leaf Rake

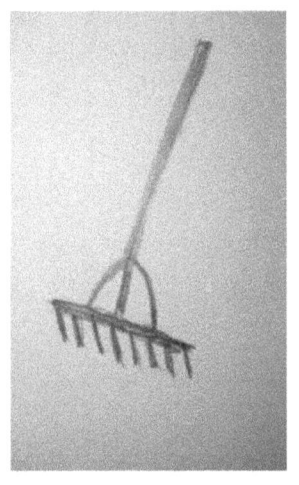  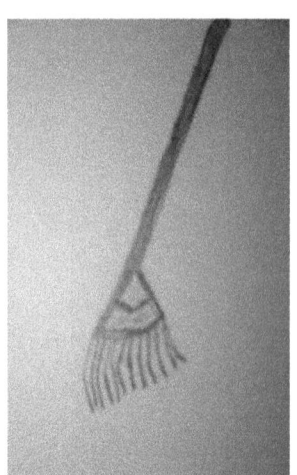

Hubert had no idea there were so many different types of tools he might need for his garden.

Hubert also found several types of wheelbarrows, flat bed wagons, and regular small wagons. He liked finding these because it is hard to carry around all the tools he would need.

Flatbed wagon

Wheelbarrow

Hubert found clay cones on a lower shelf in the back of the shed. He wondered what these were used for. He asked his friend Eddie and learned these are used to give the plants water.

WATERING:

Clay cones

Clay cone

Eddie told Hubert that clay cones and pots could be used for watering plants in the garden. Wow, Hubert said. You plant them right in the ground next to the plants and fill them with water. That must save water from evaporating in the sun, like when you use a hose or sprinkler system.

Eddie said you can even use plastic water bottles. Hubert thought that was better than throwing the plastic bottles away.

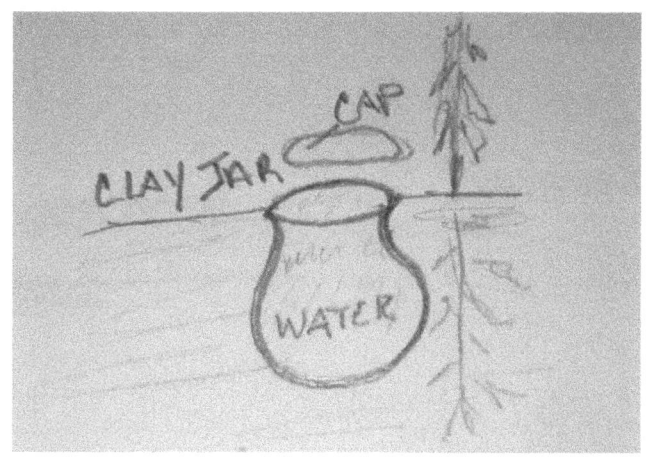

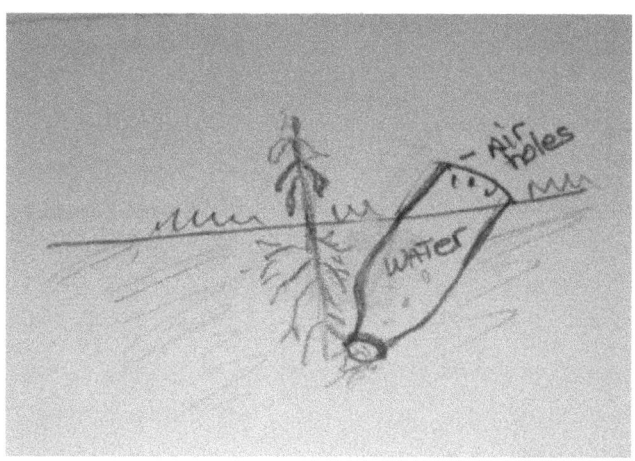

Eddie then showed Hubert different ways the garden hose, sprinkler system and watering can are used without wasting water.

The gardening hose and the watering can, can be hand-held to add water to a trench below the plants, and to fill the clay cones and pots, and the water bottles.

The sprinkler system can be run early in the morning before the sun comes up. Watering early saves water from being evaporated. Hubert thought Eddie was a very smart boy. After all, Eddie was a few years older than Hubert.

Garden hose   Watering can

Sprinkler system

Hubert thanked Eddie for explaining how these different ways of watering work, so there is no waste.

CLOSE WORK - Hand tools

The trowel, transplanter, cultivator, claw, spade, hand rake, clippers and weeder are some of the handheld tools used for close work.

Hubert went back in the shed to look at all the handheld tools. There were so many! How would he remember which tool to use, when?

Claw/Fork   Clippers

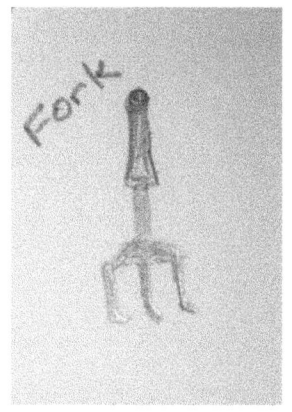   

Spade   Hand rake

Wheelbarrow - dirt, plant, tool, and waste mover

PROTECTIVE GEAR

Hubert found a wooden box with protective gear in it. There were some very dirty, and some newer hats, gloves, eye gear, bandanas, sun protection lotion and full water bottles. He thought that it was very smart to have these things handy. He didn't want to get hurt. There was also a first aid kit in case he did cut himself.

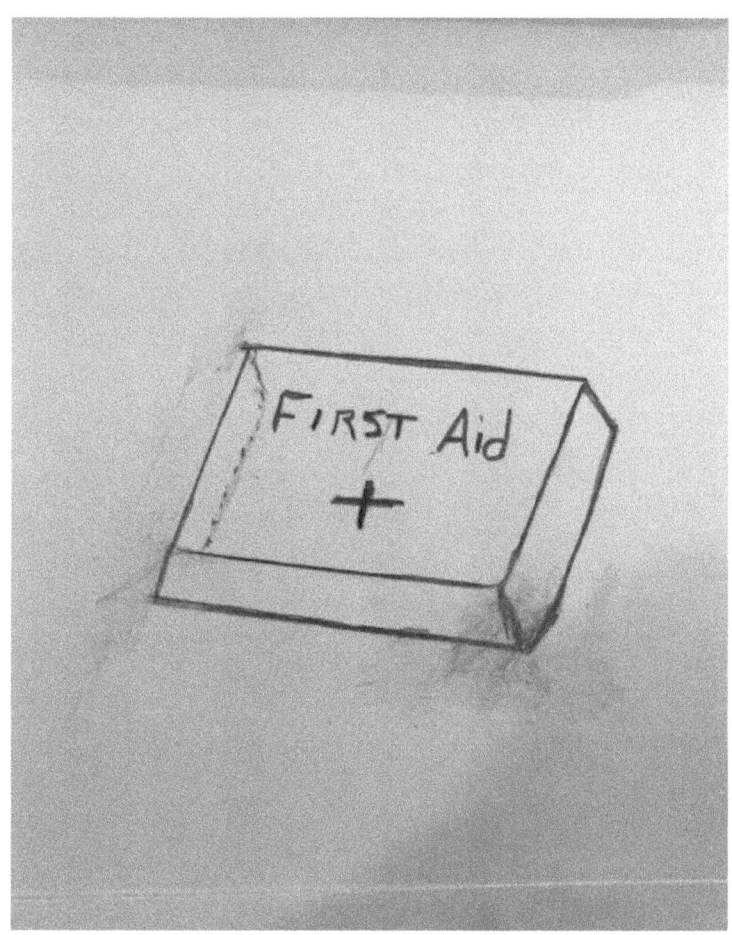

PROTECTIVE GEAR

Gardening Gloves protect hands and fingers

Hats, Sunscreen, Bandanas and Water:

Hat　　　　　　　Sunscreen

Bandanas

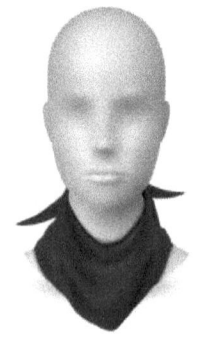 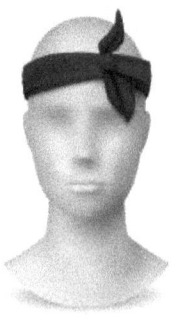 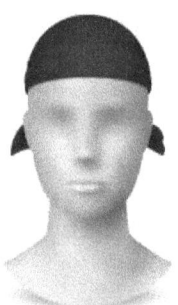 

Water

Protective eye covering

CHAPTER 2: FERTILIZING AND COMPOSTING

Fertilizer: (if not composting):

There were so many types of fertilizer's that Hubert was confused. His friend Eddie had to explain the different types of fertilizer, how to use them, and when to use them. Eddie said it is very important to read the directions on the fertilizer bag or box, because fertilizer can poison a person if handled wrong. Also, too much fertilizer can burn or kill your plants.

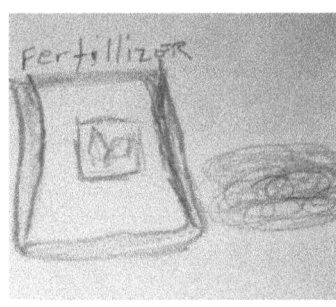
Fertilizer bag

Hand fertilizing

Composting

Create a natural fertilizer by composting. Create a composting space away from the garden and house. Section the space off.

Hubert did not know what composting was, or how to do it. When Eddie explained composting to him, Hubert thought it was a brilliant idea to use waste foods and worms to create rich dirt for planting.

All composting requires four basic ingredients:

Brown waste, Green waste, Dirt, Water

- Use equal quantity of greens to browns
- Too much green waste can cause lots of maggots. Add more brown waste.
- Alternate layers of organic materials of different-sized particles.

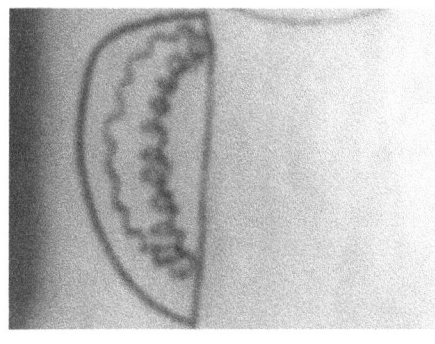

Eli Tracewell

Eli Tracewell

Eddie told Hubert to be sure to keep the animals out of the compost pile. It's best to have a barrier or fence around the compost pile or have it in a barrel so animals can't get in, except the worms you put in it. Hubert thought this was funny and laughed. Eddie said he sounded like a donkey.

- Cover each layer of green and brown waste with dirt
- Water and turn over frequently

- Allow to decay over time. Continue adding to it. Spread on your garden and work into the dirt when preparing your garden.

What NOT Too Compost

1. No Black walnut tree leaves, hulls, or twigs
2. No charcoal or wood ash
3. No diseased or insect infected plants
4. No fats, grease, oils
5. No meat or meat bones, or fish or fish bones
6. No pet or human waste
7. No cat litter
8. Nothing treated with chemical pesticides, or any type of chemicals.

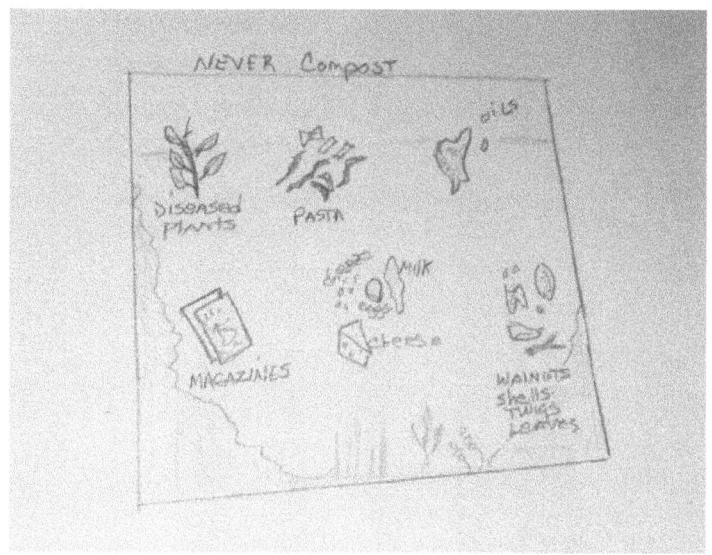

9. Do not put dairy or meat in the compost pile.

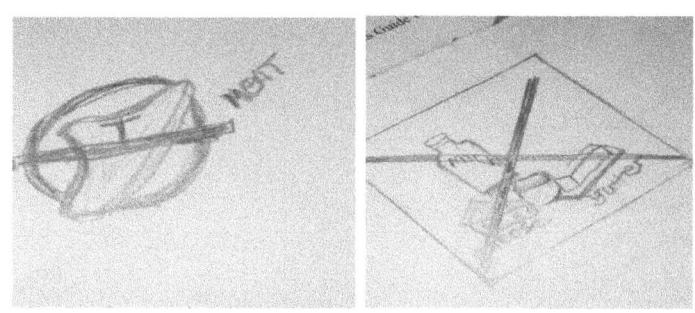

What to include in the compost pile:

- **Greens** - Include materials like:
    a. grass clippings, vegetable waste, fruit scraps, eggshells
    b. coffee grounds, coffee filters, tea bags
    c. old bread, pasta, dough
    d. left over non-meat or non-dairy food
- Green materials provide nitrogen.

- **Browns** - Includes materials like:
    a. dead leaves, branches, twigs, wood chips, nut shells,
    b. shredded newspaper, other paper, cut up cardboard
    c. yard trimmings, grass clippings, old or dead (non-diseased) plants, leaves,
    d. sawdust, hay, straw, cut up old cotton or wool rugs, fireplace ash, hair, fur.
- **Worms** - Add worms to the compost pile for added waste and aeration.
- Brown materials provide carbon for your compost.

Turn the mixture over periodically to allow air to enter.

Hubert asked Eddie where he could put food waste before he adds it to the compost pile. Eddie laughed and said put it in a bucked with a cover.

Eddie said "don't leave it in the house too long though. It might start to smell. You should empty it in the compost pile and then rinse the pail out every couple of days." Hubert made a funny face and said, he would remember to empty it often.

Water the compost pile often

Farm animal pictures

Hen House

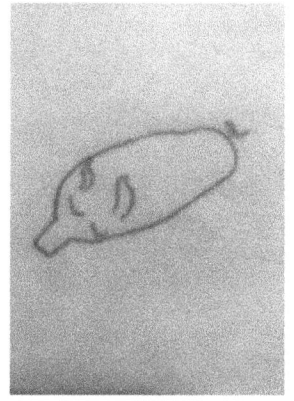

Shovel compost onto the garden. Add about 1-2" of compost to soil preparation, before planting. Work into the regular soil.

Creating Compost Tea - Runoff from the compost pile

Hubert thought it was funny that you make compost tea for the garden. He didn't know gardens drank tea.

- Before building your compost pile, scrape out several rows in the ground.
- Put PVC pipe, cut in half length wise, in the rows. This will collect the runoff.
- Dig a larger hole to put a bucket in and have the PVC ends dropping into the bucket.
- The bucket will collect the runoff – called compost tea. Use this runoff as fertilizer.

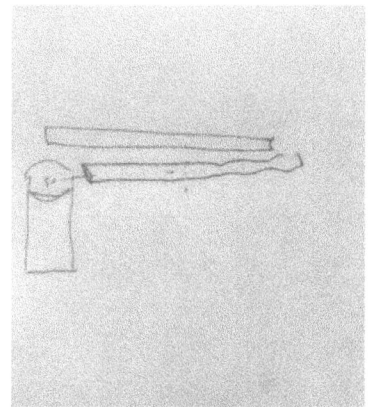
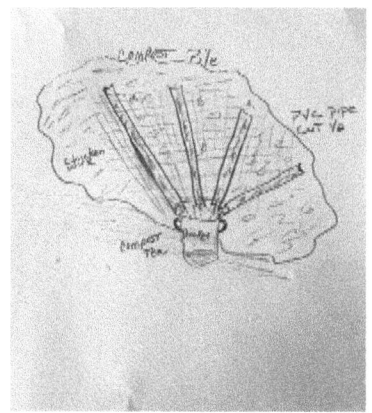

Water garden with weed water

Wow! Hubert said. You can use the wastewater from the compost pile to water the garden. It must smell. Eddie said that it did but is very good for the garden. He then told Hubert that he can make other types of compost tea by using buckets and pillowcases.

Hubert was confused. A pillowcase? Eddie said yes. Put the grass clippings and weeds in the pillowcase. Put pillowcase in a bucket of water to soak. Then after a few weeks of the water soaking the weeds, you pull out the pillowcase, throw it away, and the water left in the bucket is good for watering your garden. Well, I never would have thought to do that said Hubert.

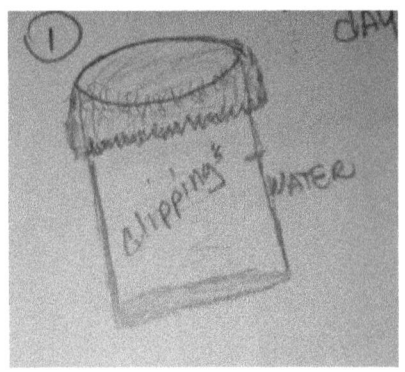 

Greens Tea:

- In a 5 gallon or larger container place an old pillowcase

    Bucket with pillowcase inside

- Fill the bucked ½ to ¾ water
- After raking up yard clippings and other organic matter such as leaves, flowers, garden leftovers, place the items in the pillowcase
- Continue adding to this. Let it soak for at least a week
- When you are ready, remove the pillowcase and discard
- Water the garden with this nutrient rich water

Weed Tea:

- In a 5 gallon or larger container place an old pillowcase
- Fill the bucked ½ to ¾ water
- Collect weeds from your yard and place the items in the pillowcase
- Continue adding to this. Let soak for at least a week
- When you are ready, remove the pillowcase and discard
- Water the garden with this nutrient rich water

DO NOT INCLUDE DISEASED ORGANIC MATTER

Chapter Three: Preparing and cultivating the soil

There are many types of soil. Some soil is sandy, other soils are heavy clay, some are rocky, some are rich in nutrients. The pH of some soil is too acid, or the soil is too alkaline. Some soil is full of caliche, other soil is too wet. The soil may be very hard, difficult to dig.

Before you begin soil preparation, have your County Agriculture Extension Department (every county has one) analyze your soil and make recommendations for improving your soil. Follow their recommendations for enriching the soil for planting.

Preparation

- Test the pH of the soil and add the right chemicals to improving the soil.

pH soil tester

- Work with the County Agriculture Extension office to improve the soil if needed
- Rototill the dirt or dig about 4-6" deep

- Break up any clods and remove any rocks and other debris.

- Rake out the soil until it is smooth

Add 2-3 inches of compost to the dirt and work into soil.

- Water the soil for 2-3 days to stimulate the compost
- When the garden is ready, Hoe furrows about 4-6 inches deep in garden area

Planting

- Plant seeds according to manufacturer instructions, or
- Plant starter plants according to directions
- Water daily but don't drown your garden
- Weed as needed and put the weeds into the weed tea container

Don't forget the scarecrow

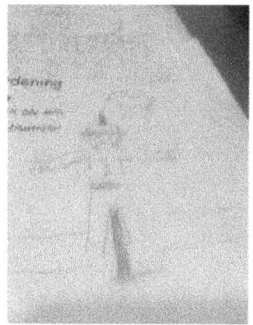

Cultivating the soil

- Weed often and put the weeds into the weed tea bucket
- Hoe or rake around the plant rows to aerate the soil.

- Water daily, if possible, but do not drown your garden.
- Add one of the "tea" concoctions to garden about every

3 - 4 weeks

- Lightly work into the soil around the plants

Chapter Four:
Planting from Seeds, or Transplanting Starter Plants

Planting

- cultivate the soil and plant in the ground
- plant in raised bed planter boxes
- plant in containers
- put 2-4" holes in PVC pipe, hang the pipes, and plant in the holes
- plant in water

Focusing on in-ground planting

- Draw out your garden on graph paper, to scale

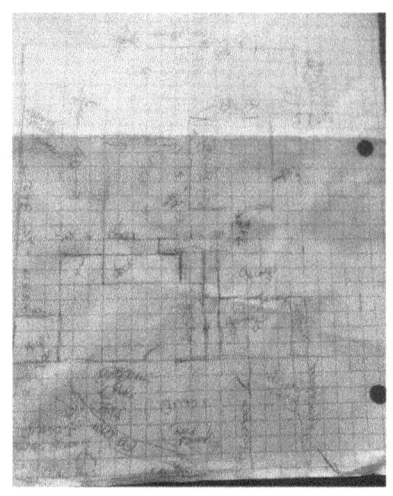

- Identify the plants you want to grow and lay out on paper, in the garden plot you created. Be sure to plant seeds or starter plants far enough apart so they can grow.

   Radish

Tomato

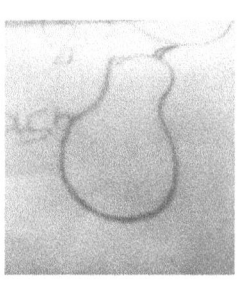   Squash

   Spinach

   Sweet Potato

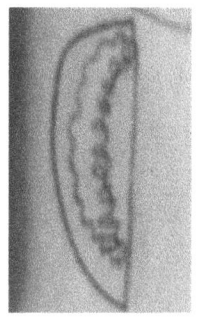   Watermelon

 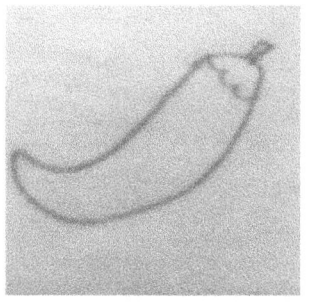 

Pumpkin Pepper Turnip

  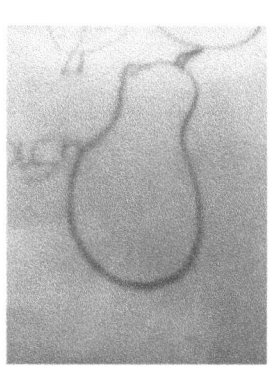

Radish Onions Squash

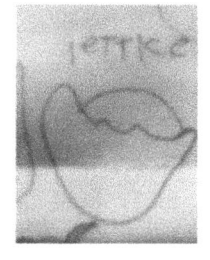  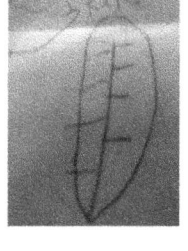 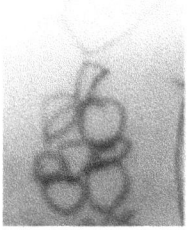

Lettuce Broccoli Kale Grapes

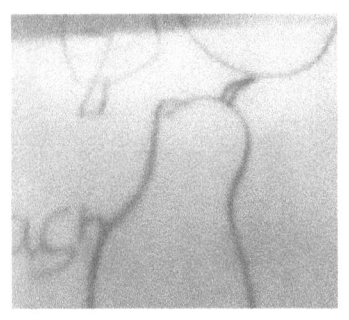  

Squash   Beets   Bell Peppers

- Identify how much growing space you will need for each item in the garden. (1 square = 12 inches or 1 foot)
- Be sure your garden is large enough before you plant

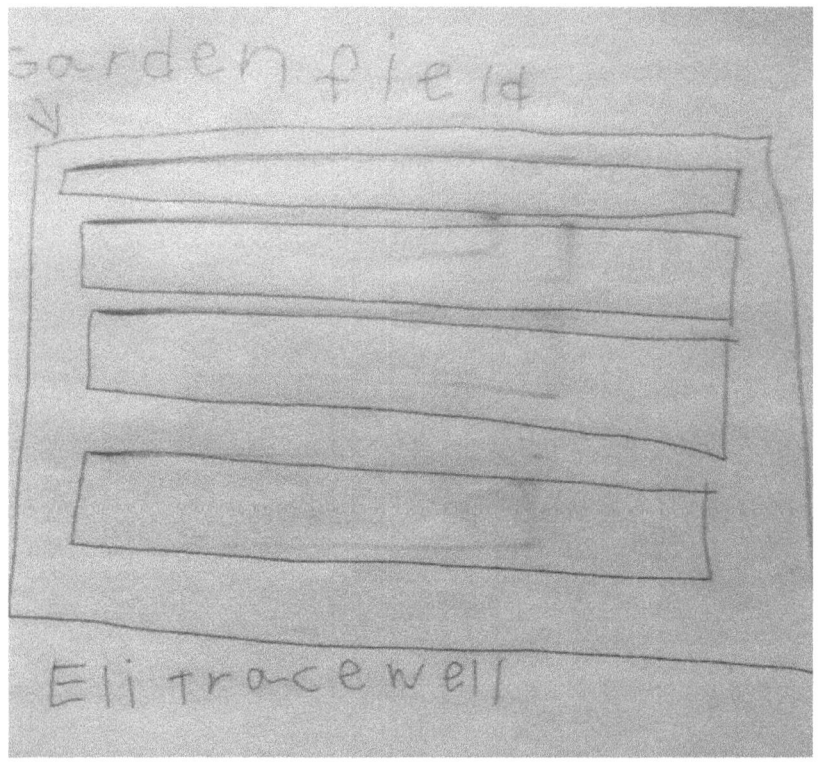

Planting from starter plants

Starting your starter plants:

- In small cups or other small containers
- Plant 2 seeds in each cup, cover with soil
- Water lightly every day
- The plant will germinate and begin to grow
- Once the plants are about 3 – 6 inches high, they are ready to transplant
- Dig holes far enough apart to place the plants in (see seed package)
- Carefully remove the plant and dirt from the small cup or other container
- Carefully place in the pre-dug holes
- Sweep surrounding soil to fill in each hole
- Pat down the soil around the plant
- Water lightly no less than every other day

Garden plant care

- Weed the garden on a regular basis
- Place weeds in weed tea mix
- With a hand tool, lightly rake and aerate around the plants to allow for air flow

Chapter Five: Harvesting and preparing for storage

Hubert was curious about what to do with all the food that he would be harvesting. He knew that he and his family would not be able to eat all of it. Eddie told him that there are a few things that he can do when the food is ripe for picking.

- Don't pick everything at the same time
- Pick and eat it fresh
- Give some to friends
- Give some to food pantries in town
- Donate to charities that collect and distribute food
- Sell at the Farmers Market in town
- Some foods can be stored in wooden boxes covered with hay, eg. squash, apples, potatoes, melons, onions, carrots, root vegetables, and more.
- Foods can be prepared for water bath canning
- Foods can be prepared for pressure canning
- Foods can be prepared for dehydrating
- Foods can be prepared for freeze drying
- Foods can be prepared for fermenting
- Foods can be prepared for freezing

Eddie said there are so many ways to preserve foods. Each way has books written about how to do each method. Eddie suggested Hubert talk to his parents about what they want to do with a big harvest.

Eddie said that they can go to the bookstore, or go online and order books that show them, step by step what to do to preserve their foods. Also, he mentioned going to Youtube. Youtube has a lot of video's about how to preserve foods.

Hubert was very excited about all that he had learned from Eddie about preparing, planting, growing, cultivating, and harvesting food.

Hubert was overwhelmed by all that there was to do. He had no idea that growing a garden took so much planning and work.

Hubert thanked Eddie for all the help he had been explaining all the steps that need to be done to grow healthy crops, and healthy farm animals.

Hubert asked Eddie to help him draw up a plan and a diagram that he could show his parents. Then he would ask his parents to help him get everything he needed to grow a small garden for the family. Eddie was very happy to help Hubert this way.

APPENDIX A: Cost of Gardening Supplies

The Cost of having a home garden: These prices give the reader an estimate of the cost of gardening. Individual prices will vary depending on where the product is purchased.

TOOLS	PRICE
Rototiller	Craftsman $200.00 ++
Flat Edge Shovel	Cobolt $30.00++
Pointed End Shovel	Craftsman $40.00++
Hoe	True Temper $20.00++
Leaf Rake	Craftsman $25.00++
Metal Rake	Cobolt $40.00++
Wheelbarrow	Cobolt $60.00++
Handheld Spade	Craftsman $15.00++
Handheld Claw	Craftsman $15.00++
Gloves	Work $8.00++
Fertilizer	Kellogg Fertilizer $40.00++ (20# bag)
Insecticides	Scotts Insecticide Killer $8.00/

bag
Post driver   Craftsman $70.00++
Planting Dirt   Range $8.00++ (5# bag)

SEED   Range $2.75 - $10.00 each
HERBS   Range $1.75 - $7.50

GARDEN AREA SUPPLIES
Wire fencing
Fencing posts
Heaters for winter planting
Tomato cages
Trellis
Wood for planter boxes
2 x 4s
½" plywood
Screws
Screening canopy
Hoses

SEED
Celery
Corn
Roman Tomatoes
Cherry Tomatoes
Beefy Tomatoes
Summer Squash

Zucchini
Cucumber
Pickling Cucumber
Watermellon
Peas
Beans
Okra

HERBS
Hot red peppers
Jalapeno peppers
Banana peppers
Garlic
Thyme
Sage
Basel
Dill
Mint
Oregano
Parsley
Endives

APPENDIX B
Preparing Your Garden for Winter

1. Test the pH of the dirt in the garden. Record it for later comparison.
2. Pull all the leftover plants and weeds out of the garden.
3. If there is food on the tree, vines, planter box, or in the ground, harvest it for later use.
4. Pull all the weeds growing in the garden spots, do not toss them in the compost pile. Either put them in the regular trash or toss them in the trash marked "outdoor vegetation", to be burned at a future date.
5. If you are making green tea, or weed tea, put the proper volume of weeds in a bucket of water. Fill the water as high as you can. Let it rest for 2 weeks. Once ready, spread it in the garden and lightly water.
6. If you have not yet added worms to your garden, now is a good time.
7. Cover the ground with one to 6 inches of compost.
8. Cover the garden space with straw, and clear or black tarp. Secure well so it does not blow way during a storm.
9. Clean the gardening equipment and store it all in the shed.
10. pH test again in the Spring before planting. Add fertil-

izer or other soil enhancers that are needed to improve the soil quality. Add new worms. Let the garden soil rest for a month before planting.

APPENDIX C
Mapping a garden area to scale

Use graph paper with 1 block = 3 feet (or more or less) Measure area to be planted (length and width). Draw area on graph paper where 1 block = 3 feet

Eg:

Area = 42 feet x 12 feet

(3'/42' = 14 blocks long)

(3'/12' = 4 blocks wide)

Mark where different types of plants will be planted.

APPENDIX D
Calculate the amount of compost needed

Determine length and width of garden area, eg: 42'x12' = 504 sq ft.

Add 3" deep compost, to be spread across the garden and rake into the dirt.

Eg.

504 sq ft x 3" = 1,512" /12" (=1 foot) - 126 ft of compost raked into the entire garden area.

Water moderately for 3 days. Plant or transplant after day 3.

About the Author

Theresa Teti is a retired public health, community health educator and a special education teacher, K - 12.

Theresa's public health career of over 25 years focused on tobacco control and tobacco cessation in the community. She brought programs into local middle schools and high schools in central California and in eastern New Mexico. Theresa also worked with teens on pregnancy prevention and teen parenting.

In 2009 Theresa obtained her New Mexico Special Education, K-12 teaching license. She later obtained a similar Arizona license.

Theresa worked as a contract special education teacher in five school districts in New Mexico and Arizona. She taught middle school and high school special education students from 2009 - July 2024.

Theresa found that her area of expertise was working with teenagers, primarily autistic students, students with traumatic brain injuries, and other challenges such as anger and behavioral issues, ticks, Tourette's, deafness and the visually impaired.

Theresa was instrumental in teaching Eli Tracewell, research assistant and illustrator of this book, ten different marketable skills over the three-year course of this project.

Although retired, Theresa continues to mentor autistic

young adults. She helped one autistic young woman create a business where she raises and sells tarantulas, and now has a YouTube channel, Sofie's Tarantula Tutorial.

Theresa now lives in southwestern New Mexico. She continues to work with autistic young adults.

Eli Tracewell is a very talented autistic young adult. He not only draws well, but he is a skilled gardener and caretaker for small farm animals. Through his relationship with Echoing Hope Ranch, Eli can help at all levels of skills in the gardens and with the animals at the Ranch. Eli is skilled in other areas as well. These skills allow Eli to help the elderly with needed repairs and yard work, as a community service project.